Sensei Self Development

Mental Health Chronicles Series

Practicing Mindfulness and Meditation

Sensei Paul David

Copyright Page

Sensei Self Development -
Practicing Mindfulness and Meditation,
by Sensei Paul David

Copyright © 2024

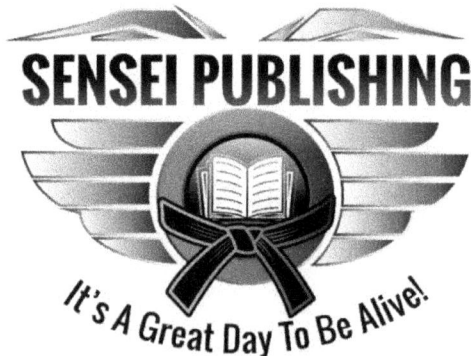

SENSEI PUBLISHING

It's A Great Day To Be Alive!

www.senseipublishing.com

@senseipublishing
#senseipublishing

Get/Share Your FREE SSD Mental Health Chronicles at
www.senseiselfdevelopment.care

or

CLICK HERE

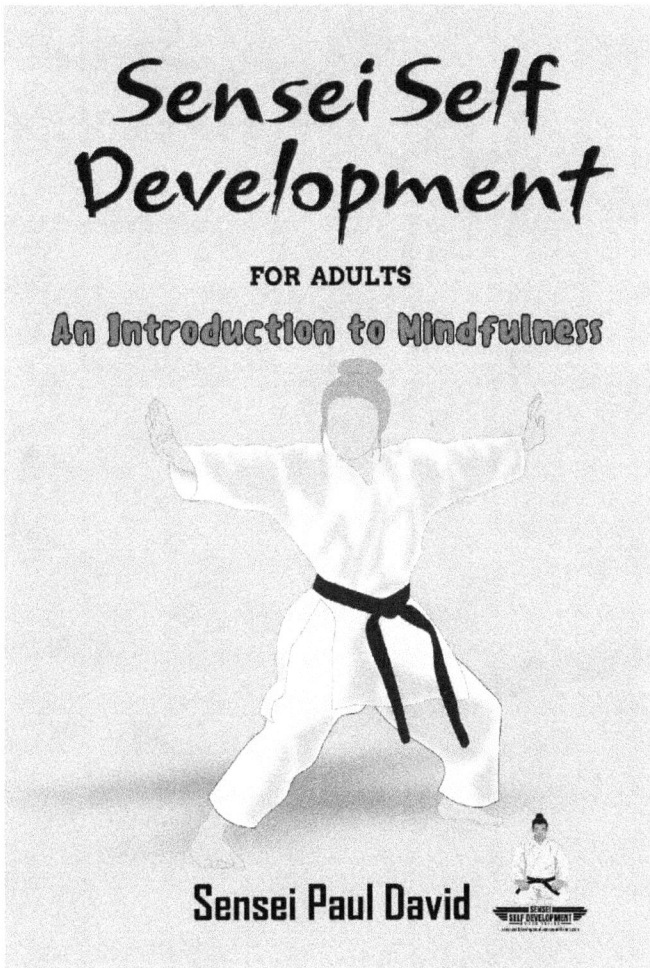

Check Out The SSD Chronicles Series CLICK HERE

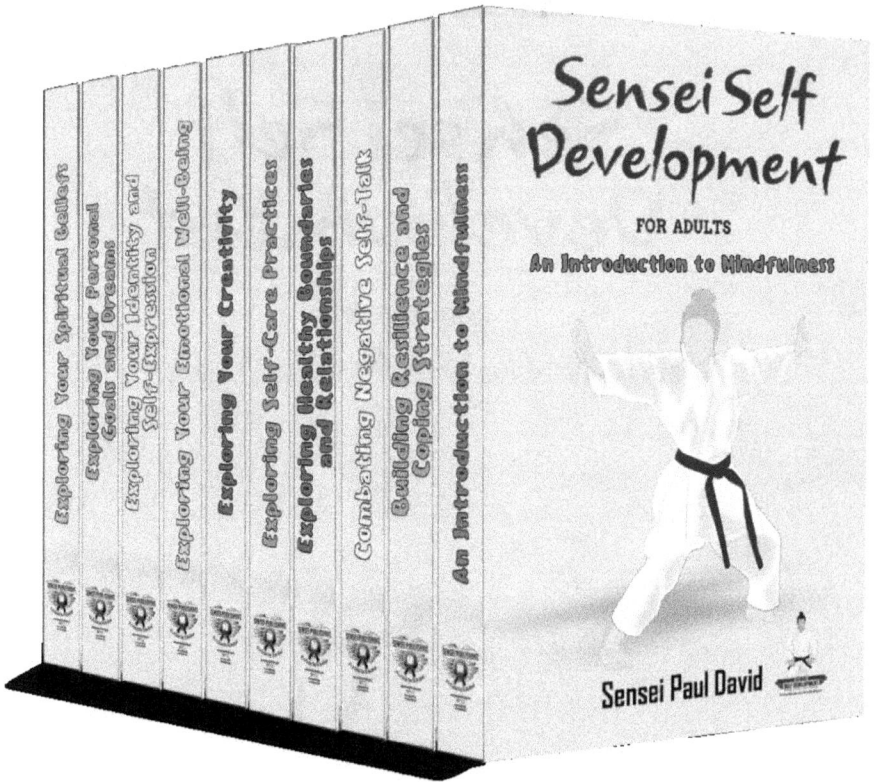

Exploring Your Spiritual Beliefs

Exploring Your Personal Goals and Dreams

Exploring Your Identity and Self-Expression

Exploring Your Emotional Well-Being

Exploring Your Creativity

Exploring Self-Care Practices

Exploring Healthy Boundaries and Relationships

Combatting Negative Self-Talk

Building Resilience and Coping Strategies

An Introduction to Mindfulness

Sensei Self Development

FOR ADULTS

An Introduction to Mindfulness

Sensei Paul David

Dedication

To those who courageously take action
towards self-improvement - you are helping to
evolve the world for generations to come.

- It's a great day to be alive!

If Found Please Contact:

_____

Reward If Found:

_____

MY COMMITMENT

I, _____
commit to writing This Sensei Self
Development Journal for at least 10 days in a
row, starting: _____

Writing this journal is valuable to me because:

_____
_____
_____
_____
_____
_____

If I finish a minimum of 10 consecutive days of
writing in this journal, I will reward myself by:

_____
_____
_____
_____

_____

_____

If I don't finish 10 days of writing this journal, I will promise to:

_____

_____

_____

_____

_____

_____

I will do the following things to ensure that I write in my Sensei Self Development Journal every day:

_____

_____

_____

_____

_____

_____

Get/Share Your FREE All-Ages Mental Health eBook Now at

www.senseiselfdevelopment.com

Or CLICK HERE

Your **Attitude** of **Gratitude**

Develop Simple Gratitude Skills for Better Living

Sensei Paul David

senseiselfdevelopment.com

Check Out Another Book In The
SSD BOOK SERIES:

senseipublishing.com/SSD_SERIES

CLICK HERE

SENSEI
SELF DEVELOPMENT
B O O K S   S E R I E S

senseiselfdevelopment.senseipublishing.com

Join Our Publishing Journey!

If you would like to receive FUTURE FREE BOOKS and get to know us better, please click www.senseipublishing.com and join our newsletter by entering your email address in the pop-up box.

Follow Our Blog: senseipauldavid.ca

Follow/Like/Subscribe: Facebook, Instagram, YouTube:
@senseipublishing

Scan the QR Code with your phone or tablet

to follow us on social media: Like / Subscribe / Follow

A Message From The Author:
Sensei Paul David

Dear Reader,

Welcome to the world of mental health journaling – a sacred space for self-reflection, growth, and healing. Within these pages, you hold the power to uplift your spirit, invigorate your mind, and nourish your goals.

In a world that often moves at blink-and-you'll-miss-it speed, it's crucial to make time for self-care and self-discovery.

Anxiety, stress, and emotional turbulence may have clouded your mind, making it difficult to find clarity and peace within. But fear not! Together, we will navigate the labyrinth of emotions, and experiences, helping to simplify the path to mental well-being.

This journal is not merely a bunch of blank pages awaiting your words. It is your compassionate companion, offering solace and understanding during your unique journey. Here, you are free to unburden yourself, celebrate small and large victories, and confront the challenges that may still linger.

Within the sheltered realm of these pages, there is no judgment, no expectation, and no pressure. Your unique experience and perspective hold immeasurable worth, and your voice deserves to be heard. Whether you choose to fill the lines with eloquence or simply scribble fragments of your thoughts, please remember each entry is a valuable contribution to your growth.

In this sacred space, you are challenged to take off the mask we so often wear in the outside world. It is here that you can be raw, vulnerable, and authentic – allowing your true self to be seen and embraced without reservation. By giving yourself permission to explore the depths of your emotions and confront the shadows that may lurk within, you will discover profound insights and find the healing you seek over time.

As you embark on this journaling journey, I encourage you to embrace the process itself rather than fixate solely on the outcome. Remember, it is not about reaching a certain destination or ticking off boxes on a list of accomplishments. Rather, it is about cultivating self-awareness, fostering self-compassion, and nurturing a sense of curiosity about the intricate workings of your intelligently beautiful mind.

In the quiet moments of reflection, let your pen become a bridge between your inner world and the possibilities that lie ahead. Create a sanctuary for your thoughts, fears, triumphs, and dreams. As you pour your heart onto these pages, allow your words to be a living testament to courage, resilience, and an unwavering commitment to your own well-being.

I am honored to be a part of your journey, and I believe in your ability to navigate the twists and turns with grace and resilience. Remember, you are not alone in this – countless others have walked similar paths, faced similar challenges, and emerged stronger and wiser on the other side. You have the power to reclaim all of your untapped joy, cultivate a positive mindset that serves you, and foster a deep sense of self-love and peaceful confident. – And it will take a worth effort and time.

So, open the first page of this journal with hope, curiosity, and an open heart and open mind. Embrace the transformative power of self-reflection, and allow it to guide you towards a life of greater fulfilment and peace. Each journaling session is an opportunity to not only connect with yourself but also to rekindle the light within that sometimes flickers but never extinguishes.

Remember, the pages you are about to fill are not just a record of your journey but also a testament to your strength, resilience, and indomitable spirit. Cherish this space, invest in yourself, and let your words be an ode to the magnificent journey of becoming whole.

With great respect for your decision to evolve,

Paul

MY CONVICTION

Please circle your answers below

I am DECIDING to be patient with myself and this PROCESS each time I journal toward my improved state of mental well-being

YES   NO

"The present moment is filled with joy and happiness. If you are attentive,
you will see it."

Thich Nhat Hanh

Introduction

Mindfulness and Meditation

When we see someone walking down the street talking to themselves, we might think they're mentally ill, especially if they're not wearing a headset. But, really, all of us engage in this kind of self-talk. The difference is, most of us do it silently, without mumbling. We replay past conversations in our minds, thinking about what we said, what we didn't, and what we wish we'd said. We also imagine future scenarios, filled with words and images that either lift us up with hope or weigh us down with fear.

This internal narration of the present might seem odd, but it's quite normal. We silently comment on our observations and experiences, like "That's a nice desk. I wonder what kind of wood that is. Oh, but it has no drawers. How can you have a desk without at least one drawer?" In these moments, we're talking to ourselves, not to someone else. We may act like keeping these thoughts internal signifies mental stability. But does it? It's a question worth asking. Maybe we are all a little ill, walking around talking to ourselves in our mind, the only difference being we are not talking loudly.

I am a jiu-jitsu instructor. When I first began teaching, I had rented a shabby gymnasium. I was young, I had tough times and I would sleep on the office floor.

The first sign of trouble was a subtle leak in a seldom-used storage area of the gym. Finding the leak almost felt like a stroke of luck, given how easily it could have gone unnoticed. A plumber promptly fixed it, followed by a swift patch-up of the ceiling. "These things happen," I told myself.

But the sense of calm was short-lived. Just a few days later, another leak appeared, this time in the main training area. I called the same plumber with a mix of annoyance and a sinking feeling of what might come next.

A month later, the real turmoil began. A major pipe burst in the gym, turning the mats and training area into a waterlogged mess. The repair process was extensive and disruptive, filling the gym with dust and debris. Professional cleaners were brought in, their vacuums and mops working overtime. We had to forgo heating to prevent dust from spreading through the gym's ventilation system.

Eventually, the gym was restored to its former glory. But the respite was brief. Just a month after these extensive repairs, the familiar, dreaded sound of water dripping resurfaced. I was in my makeshift bed in my office when I heard it, and in an instant, I was up, a mix of disbelief and frustration washing over me. The sight of a new, bulging leak in the ceiling confirmed my fears – the gym, my sanctuary and occasional resting place, was facing yet another round of disruption.

Of course, a jiu-jitsu gym, like any physical space, is at the mercy of natural laws—it won't mend itself. The moment I started scrambling for buckets and containers to catch the incessant drip of water, I was simply reacting to an unavoidable physical reality. However, my inner turmoil was entirely a creation of my own mind. Regardless of the immediate demands, I had a choice: I could address each issue with calm, patience, and focus, or I could let myself be overwhelmed by panic. Each moment of the day – and indeed, every moment of life – presents a chance to either approach challenges with a composed mindset or to succumb to unnecessary distress.

We can tackle mental anguish of this sort on two different levels. One way is to counterbalance it with positive thoughts, and the other is to transcend thought entirely. The first method doesn't require any meditation experience and can be highly effective with the right mindset. It's what many refer to as "looking on the bright side."

For example, as I felt my frustration mounting like a tempest, my colleague at the gym pointed out that we should be grateful that it was only fresh water leaking from the ceiling, not sewage. This perspective was strikingly grounding. I could almost tangibly sense the relief of dealing with clean water rather than wading through a far worse scenario. It was indeed a relief!

I frequently employ such thoughts to dislodge my mind from the trenches of needless suffering. Had it been sewage cascading from the gym's ceiling, what price would I have willingly paid to turn it into mere water? Probably a lot.

Another approach to managing mental stress is through mindfulness and meditation. These practices help us to step away from our thoughts completely.

Let me explain.

We often let negative emotions linger longer than necessary. When we get angry, we don't just feel anger momentarily; we sustain it by engaging in thoughts that fuel the fire. We replay the reasons for our anger, like remembering an insult or thinking about what we should have said. What we often fail to recognize is the active role we play in maintaining these emotions. Without continually feeding these thoughts, staying angry for more than a few moments is almost impossible.

While meditation might not prevent you from getting angry, it can help you learn not to remain in that state for long. And when considering the impact of anger, the difference between moments and hours, or even days, is profound.

Even without meditation experience, most people have had their negative emotions interrupted suddenly. For example, you might be extremely angry, but then an important phone call forces you to shift gears and put on a sociable demeanor. This sudden change from a negative state to a more neutral or positive one is a common experience. However, we often find ourselves entangled in negative emotions again at the first opportunity. It's important to become aware of these interruptions.

Maybe you're feeling down, but then something makes you laugh, or you're impatient in traffic until a call from a friend brightens your mood. These instances are like natural experiments in changing emotions. Noticing that focusing on something else can lead to a different emotional state shows how quickly our mood can shift. These moments are glimpses of what it's like to be free from our habitual reactions.

The reality is that you don't need to wait for a distraction to change your mood. You can observe your negative feelings directly, without judgment or resistance. Ask yourself: What is anger? Where do you feel it in your body? How does it arise moment by moment? And what part of you is noticing these feelings? By exploring these questions mindfully, you'll find that negative emotions often dissipate on their own.

Thinking is crucial for us. It's vital for forming beliefs, making plans, learning, moral reasoning, and other human capabilities. It underpins our social relationships, cultural norms, and even science. However, our tendency to overly identify with our thoughts – not recognizing them just as fleeting elements in our consciousness – is a major cause of suffering.

Try an experiment: see if you can stop thinking for the next sixty seconds. You can focus on your breathing or listen to the sounds around you, like birds chirping. The key is to not get swept up in any thought, even for a moment. Put this book aside for a minute and give it a try.

Some of you might find yourselves so caught up in thoughts that you believe you've succeeded in stopping them. New meditators often think they can focus on something simple, like their breath, for several minutes. But after some time of intense practice, they realize their attention gets hijacked by thoughts every few seconds. This is a sign of progress. It requires a certain level of focus just to become aware of how easily we get distracted. In reality, even if I put a gun to your head or gave you a million dollars, you couldn't go a full minute without any thoughts.

This reveals a fascinating aspect of the human mind. We're capable of extraordinary understanding and creativity, and can withstand immense challenges. Yet, we can't just stop our internal dialogue on command, regardless of the stakes. We can't even consistently recognize each thought as it surfaces without getting sidetracked by them.

Without extensive meditation practice, staying fully aware of anything for a full minute is simply beyond our reach. We spend much of our lives engulfed in thought.

What should we make of this fact? In Western culture, it's often overlooked. But in Eastern traditions, particularly in contemplative practices like Buddhism, being constantly distracted by thoughts is seen as the root of human suffering. From this perspective, being lost in any kind of thought, whether pleasant or painful, is like being asleep and dreaming. It's a state of being unaware of what's truly happening in the present moment, almost like a psychosis.

The problem isn't necessarily the thoughts themselves, but our identification with them. Believing we are the thinker of our thoughts – not seeing each thought as just a fleeting event in our consciousness – is a delusion that leads to much of our conflict and unhappiness. It doesn't matter if your mind is occupied with complex problems in mathematics or medical research; if you're thinking without being aware of it, you're confused about your true identity.

The practice of mindfulness and meditation serves to break free from the enthrallment of our thoughts. So we can watch our thoughts pass by untethered from us, without affecting our equanimity.

Difference between Mindfulness and Meditation

Mindfulness and meditation are interrelated yet distinct concepts.

Meditation encompasses a range of practices designed to enhance concentration, clarity, emotional positivity, and an insightful understanding of reality. These practices often involve focusing on something specific, such as an object, a thought, or an activity, to sharpen attention and awareness. There are various forms of meditation, including sitting in silence, chanting mantras, or concentrating on one's breathing.

Mindfulness, in contrast, is a state of being that can be integrated into meditation but also extends into everyday life. It's about being completely immersed in the present, observing your thoughts and feelings without getting sidetracked or making judgments. Mindfulness can be practiced in ordinary activities like eating, walking, or even while engaging in conversation. It doesn't require a designated time, posture, or environment.

To sum it up, meditation is typically a more structured practice that often incorporates mindfulness, whereas mindfulness is a continuous approach that can be applied to all facets of day-to-day life.

Fast Facts

1. Stress Reduction Mechanisms: Meditation helps in stress reduction by activating the body's relaxation response through the parasympathetic nervous system. This counteracts the body's fight or flight response, reducing the release of stress hormones like cortisol and adrenaline, leading to a decrease in heart rate, blood pressure, and muscle tension.

2. Improving Focus and Attention: Meditation practices, especially those involving focused attention on an object, sound, or the breath, have been shown to increase the thickness of the prefrontal cortex. This brain region is associated with higher-order brain functions like concentration, decision-making, and

awareness, leading to improved cognitive abilities.

3. Emotional Regulation and Mood Enhancement: Mindfulness meditation encourages practitioners to observe their thoughts and feelings without judgment. This practice helps in distancing oneself from negative thought patterns, reducing the impact of emotional volatility and mood swings. It increases activity in the brain's regions associated with positive emotions and decreases activity in areas related to negativity.

4. Physical Health Benefits:

- Blood Pressure: Meditation induces relaxation, which prompts the release of nitric oxide in the blood vessels, dilating them and lowering blood pressure.

- Chronic Pain: Mindfulness can change the way one perceives pain by altering the brain's pain pathways and increasing pain tolerance.

- Sleep: Meditation can enhance the relaxation response at night, making it easier to fall and stay asleep.

5. Neurological Benefits: Regular meditation can lead to neuroplasticity, where the brain forms new connections and changes its structure. It can increase gray matter density in areas of the brain related to learning, memory, and emotion regulation, and decrease the size of the amygdala, which is responsible for fear, anxiety, and stress.

6. Mindfulness in Daily Life: Practicing mindfulness in everyday activities helps individuals to engage fully in the moment, leading to greater enjoyment and fulfillment in those activities. It can also improve the ability to manage stress in real-time and reduce the tendency towards automatic negative reactions.

7. Mental Health Management: For anxiety and depression, mindfulness-based interventions can help break the cycle of negative thoughts, emotions, and body sensations, reducing the recurrence of depressive episodes and mitigating the symptoms of anxiety disorders.

8. Enhancing Creativity: Meditation can foster a state of mind that allows for greater creative thinking by reducing the mental chatter and distractions that often inhibit our creative processes.

9. Building Community and Social Skills: Group meditation practices can enhance feelings of social connectedness, reducing feelings of loneliness and social isolation. They can also improve empathy and compassion, both towards oneself and others, enhancing overall social relationships.

In summary, the benefits of meditation and mindfulness are profound and diverse, impacting not only mental health but also physical health, cognitive functions, emotional regulation, social skills, and overall life satisfaction.

How to Practise Mindfulness

1. Basic Mindfulness Exercise

First, let's begin with the most basic mindfulness practice.

1. Find a Quiet Place: Choose a quiet and comfortable place where you can sit or lie down without being disturbed.

2. Adopt a Comfortable Posture: Sit or lie down in a comfortable position. You can sit on a chair with your feet flat on the ground, on a cushion, or on the floor with your legs crossed. Keep your back straight but relaxed.

3. Focus on Your Breath: Gently close your eyes and bring your attention to your breath. Notice the sensation of air entering and leaving

your nostrils, or the rise and fall of your chest or abdomen.

4. Be Present: If your mind wanders, which is natural, gently acknowledge it and bring your focus back to your breath. The key is not to judge yourself but to observe your thoughts as they come and go.

5. Expand Your Awareness: Gradually, expand your awareness from your breath to your body. Notice any tension or relaxation in different parts of your body. Be aware of any sensations, thoughts, or feelings that arise.

6. Practice Regularly: Try to practice mindfulness daily, even if it's just for a few minutes. The more you practice, the easier it will become to bring this sense of calm and presence into your everyday life.

Remember, mindfulness is about being present and fully engaged with whatever you are doing at the moment, without judgment or distraction.

2. Mindful Eating

Mindful eating is a practice that involves being fully present and engaged with the experience of eating. It's about savoring each bite, noticing the flavors, textures, and sensations of your food, and listening to your body's hunger and fullness cues. This approach to eating can transform meals into a source of pleasure and mindfulness, rather than a rushed or mindless activity.

When practicing mindful eating, you're encouraged to slow down and eat without distraction. This means turning off the TV, putting away your phone, and really focusing on your meal. Take small bites, chew thoroughly, and really taste your food. Notice the aroma, the flavors that emerge as you chew, and the texture of the food in your mouth.

Mindful eating also involves being aware of your body's hunger and satiety signals. It's about eating when you're truly hungry and stopping when you're comfortably full, rather than eating out of boredom, stress, or habit. This can lead to a healthier relationship with food, as you learn to eat for nourishment and satisfaction, rather than as an emotional response.

This practice not only enhances the enjoyment of your meals but can also lead to better digestion, as eating slowly and thoroughly chewing helps your body to process food more effectively. Additionally, it can be a helpful tool for those looking to develop a healthier eating pattern, as it encourages you to make more conscious food choices.

3. Mindful Walking

Our mind naturally wanders, and in mindfulness practices, mantras help in anchoring our thoughts. A mantra, which can be a word or phrase, is repeated silently or aloud during mindfulness meditation. This repetition serves as a gentle tool to bring the wandering mind back to the present moment.

For me, walking acts like a mantra. It keeps my focus into the present. As you step out of your house for a walk, you pause for a moment, taking a deep breath. This is your time to connect with the present moment. You set an intention to be fully aware during your walk, leaving behind any distractions or worries.

With the first few steps, you focus on the sensation of your feet touching the ground. You feel the gentle pressure on the soles of your shoes as they meet the earth, a rhythmic motion that anchors you in the here and now. Each step becomes a conscious interaction with the world around you.

You notice the gentle breeze against your skin, the subtle shifts in temperature. Perhaps it's the warmth of the sun or the cool shade under a tree. These sensations, often overlooked, become vivid and meaningful.

As you walk, your eyes take in the surroundings. Maybe it's the vibrant green of the leaves, the intricate patterns of the bark on the trees, or the dance of light and shadow on the path ahead. You observe these details with a sense of curiosity and wonder, as if seeing them for the first time.

Your ears tune in to the sounds around you. The distant chirping of birds, the rustle of leaves underfoot, the rhythmic pattern of your own breath. Each sound adds a layer to your experience, creating a symphony that is both calming and invigorating.

Throughout your walk, your mind may wander, pulled away by thoughts or distractions. When this happens, you gently guide your attention back to the sensations of walking – the feel of the ground, the sights, the sounds. This return to the present moment is done without judgment, acknowledging that the wandering mind is simply part of the human experience.

As you near the end of your walk, you slow down, taking a moment to reflect on the journey. You realize that what could have been just a simple walk has turned into a nourishing practice, leaving you feeling grounded, calm, and connected. This is the essence of mindful walking – a simple yet profound way to engage with the world in a more meaningful, present, and connected manner.

***

Mindfulness is an adaptable practice. It's the art of being fully present in the moment, whatever and wherever that moment might be. This practice isn't confined to quiet meditation rooms or serene natural settings; it's equally at home in the hustle and bustle of city streets, in the midst of a busy workday, or during the simple acts of household chores.

Picture yourself in any ordinary moment – perhaps washing dishes, waiting in line, or walking to work. In these moments, mindfulness invites you to shift your attention to the here and now. As you focus on your breath, the sensations in your body, or the sights and sounds around you, you create a space of calm awareness amidst the day's activities.

By anchoring yourself in the now, mindfulness allows your mind to take a break from the past or future worries that often fuel anxiety and stress.

Regularly practicing mindfulness cultivates a sense of calm and balance, making you less reactive to stress triggers. This shift doesn't happen overnight, but with consistent practice, you'll find a noticeable decrease in anxiety and stress levels and an increase in feelings of peace and well-being.

How to Practise Meditation

To begin a meditation session, find a comfortable position, sitting with your spine straight, either on a chair or cross-legged on a cushion. Close your eyes, take a few deep breaths, and become aware of the points where your body contacts the chair or floor. Notice the sensations that arise from sitting – whether it's pressure, warmth, tingling, or vibration.

Next, shift your focus to your breathing. Observe the breath where it feels most prominent, either at your nostrils or as your abdomen rises and falls. Let your attention rest on the sensation of breathing, allowing the breath to flow naturally without trying to control it.

As you concentrate on breathing, your mind will inevitably wander. When this happens, gently guide your attention back to the breath. Throughout this process, you'll become aware of various sounds, bodily sensations, or emotions. Simply observe these as they occur, acknowledging their presence without getting entangled in them, and then return your focus to your breath.

Whenever you catch yourself lost in thought, take a moment to observe the thought itself as an object of consciousness. After acknowledging it, bring your attention back to the breath, or to any sounds or sensations that arise in the next moment.

Continue this practice, aiming to simply witness all objects of consciousness – be it sights, sounds, sensations, emotions, or thoughts – as they come and go.

For those new to meditation, it can be helpful to have these instructions spoken aloud during your session. There are countless meditation guides available for free on YouTube you can try.

Before We Get Started…

Remember, mindfulness journaling is a personal practice, and these questions are meant to guide and inspire you. Feel free to adapt and modify them to suit your needs and preferences. Explore, reflect, and embrace the opportunity to deepen your self-awareness and cultivate a sense of inner peace.

Date ___ / ___ / ___ : S M T W Th F S

I feel:
(please circle)

because   because   because   because   because
_____   _____   _____   _____   _____
_____   _____   _____   _____   _____

Today I Am Grateful For

1. _____
2. _____
3. _____

What could help transform today into a remarkable day?

Reflective Writing

What have I learned about myself while practicing mindfulness and meditation?

_____

_____

_____

_____

_____

_____

_____

What is the primary goal of mindfulness practice?

A) Improving future planning
B) Enhancing present-moment awareness
C) Avoiding negative emotions
D) Achieving a state of relaxation

All Are Correct - Choose The Response You Feel Is Most Important To Remember

Date ___ / ___ / ___ : S M T W Th F S

I feel:
(please circle)

because because because because because
_____ _____ _____ _____ _____
_____ _____ _____ _____ _____

Today I Am Grateful For

1. _____
2. _____
3. _____

What could help transform today into a remarkable day?

Reflective Writing

How has mindfulness and meditation helped me
become more aware of my thoughts and feelings?

_____

_____

_____

_____

_____

_____

_____

Which of the following is a common technique in mindfulness meditation?

A) Breathing exercises
B) Body scan meditation
C) Loving-kindness meditation
D) Walking meditation

All Are Correct - Choose The Response You Feel Is Most Important To Remember

Date ___ / ___ / ___: S M T W Th F S

I feel:
(please circle)

because   because   because   because   because

_____ _____ _____ _____ _____

_____ _____ _____ _____ _____

Today I Am Grateful For

1. _____
2. _____
3. _____

What could help transform today into a remarkable day?

Reflective Writing

What emotions do I typically experience during mindfulness and meditation practice?

_____

_____

_____

_____

_____

_____

_____

_____

Mindfulness can help reduce the symptoms of which of the following conditions?

A) Anxiety
B) Depression
C) Chronic pain
D) Stress

All Are Correct - Choose The Response You Feel Is Most Important To Remember

Date ___ / ___ / ___ : S   M   T   W   Th   F   S

I feel:
(please circle)

because _____ because _____ because _____ because _____ because _____

Today I Am Grateful For

1. _____
2. _____
3. _____

What could help transform today into a remarkable day?

Reflective Writing

How does mindfulness and meditation help me manage stress and difficult emotions?

_____

_____

_____

_____

_____

_____

_____

Which element is typically part of a body scan meditation?

A) Focusing on each body part sequentially

B) Judging sensations

C) Ignoring discomfort

D) Enhancing awareness of physical sensations

All Are Correct - Choose The Response You Feel Is Most Important To Remember

Date ___ / ___ / ___ : S   M   T   W   Th   F   S

I feel:
(please circle)

because   because   because   because   because
_____ _____ _____ _____ _____
_____ _____ _____ _____ _____

Today I Am Grateful For

1. _____
2. _____
3. _____

What could help transform today into a remarkable day?

Reflective Writing

What new skills have I developed through my
mindfulness and meditation practice?

_____

_____

_____

_____

_____

_____

_____

In mindfulness practice, how should one deal with distractions?

A) Forcefully push them away
B) Gently acknowledge and return focus
C) Ignore them completely
D) Judge them and analyze their importance

All Are Correct - Choose The Response You Feel Is Most Important To Remember

Date ___ / ___ / ___ : S   M   T   W   Th   F   S

I feel:
(please circle)

because   because   because   because   because
_____   _____   _____   _____   _____
_____   _____   _____   _____   _____

Today I Am Grateful For

1. _____
2. _____
3. _____

What could help transform today into a remarkable day?

Reflective Writing

How has mindfulness and meditation helped me become
more aware of my body?

_____

_____

_____

_____

_____

_____

_____

Which of the following is NOT a common form of meditation?

A) Guided meditation
B) Transcendental meditation
C) Visualization meditation
D) Memorization meditation

All Are Correct - Choose The Response You Feel Is Most Important To Remember

Date ___ / ___ / ___: S M T W Th F S

I feel:
(please circle)

because   because   because   because   because
_____   _____   _____   _____   _____
_____   _____   _____   _____   _____

Today I Am Grateful For

1. _____
2. _____
3. _____

What could help transform today into a remarkable day?

Reflective Writing

How has my practice of mindfulness and meditation changed over time?

_____

_____

_____

_____

_____

_____

_____

_____

What is a mantra in meditation?

A) A relaxing sound
B) A repetitive word or phrase
C) A type of visualization
D) A breathing technique

All Are Correct - Choose The Response You Feel Is Most Important
To Remember

Date ___ / ___ / ___ : S   M   T   W   Th   F   S

I feel:
(please circle)

because   because   because   because   because

_____   _____   _____   _____   _____
_____   _____   _____   _____   _____

Today I Am Grateful For

1. _____
2. _____
3. _____

What could help transform today into a remarkable day?

Reflective Writing

What is the most difficult aspect of mindfulness and meditation for me?

_____

_____

_____

_____

_____

_____

_____

_____

Which practice involves sending thoughts of love and kindness to oneself and others?

A) Mindful eating

B) Loving-kindness meditation (Metta)

C) Zen meditation

D) Body scan meditation

All Are Correct - Choose The Response You Feel Is Most Important To Remember

Date ___ / ___ / ___: S   M   T   W   Th   F   S

I feel:
(please circle)

because   because   because   because   because

_____ _____ _____ _____ _____

_____ _____ _____ _____ _____

Today I Am Grateful For

1. _____

2. _____

3. _____

What could help transform today into a remarkable day?

Reflective Writing

How has mindfulness and meditation impacted my relationships?

_____

_____

_____

_____

_____

_____

_____

_____

Which of the following is true about mindful breathing?

A) It requires special equipment
B) It focuses on controlling breath speed
C) It is about observing the breath without altering it
D) It involves holding the breath for extended periods

All Are Correct - Choose The Response You Feel Is Most Important To Remember

Date ___ / ___ / ___ : S M T W Th F S

I feel:
(please circle)

because _____ because _____ because _____ because _____ because _____

Today I Am Grateful For

1. _____
2. _____
3. _____

What could help transform today into a remarkable day?

Reflective Writing

How has mindfulness and meditation helped me become more mindful and present in my daily life?

_____

_____

_____

_____

_____

_____

_____

_____

What can be a benefit of regular meditation practice?

A) Increased mental clarity

B) Enhanced emotional regulation

C) Improved immune function

D) Greater self-awareness

All Are Correct - Choose The Response You Feel Is Most Important To Remember

Date ___ / ___ / ___ : S   M   T   W   Th   F   S

I feel:
(please circle)

because _____   because _____   because _____   because _____   because _____

Today I Am Grateful For

1. _____
2. _____
3. _____

What could help transform today into a remarkable day?

Reflective Writing

What benefits have I experienced as a result of my mindfulness and meditation practice?

_____

_____

_____

_____

_____

_____

_____

_____

What is the "observer" or "witness" mindset in mindfulness?

A) Actively controlling thoughts
B) Observing thoughts and emotions without attachment
C) Ignoring thoughts
D) Suppressing emotions

All Are Correct - Choose The Response You Feel Is Most Important To Remember

Date ___/___/___: S   M   T   W   Th   F   S

I feel:
(please circle)

because _____   because _____   because _____   because _____   because _____
_____   _____   _____   _____   _____

Today I Am Grateful For

1. _____
2. _____
3. _____

What could help transform today into a remarkable day?

Reflective Writing

What mistakes have I made during my mindfulness and meditation practice and how can I learn from them?

_____

_____

_____

_____

_____

_____

_____

_____

Which of the following is a foundational attitude in mindfulness?

A) Curiosity
B) Patience
C) Non-striving
D) Acceptance

All Are Correct - Choose The Response You Feel Is Most Important To Remember

Date ___ / ___ / ___ : S   M   T   W   Th   F   S

I feel:
(please circle)

because   because   because   because   because
_____   _____   _____   _____   _____
_____   _____   _____   _____   _____

Today I Am Grateful For

1. _____
2. _____
3. _____

What could help transform today into a remarkable day?

Reflective Writing
What new insights have I gained from my
mindfulness and meditation practice?

_____

_____

_____

_____

_____

_____

_____

_____

What is the purpose of mindfulness-based stress reduction (MBSR)?

A) To eliminate stress completely
B) To develop a different relationship with stress
C) To avoid stressful situations
D) To promote physical fitness

All Are Correct - Choose The Response You Feel Is Most Important To Remember

Date ___ / ___ / ___ : S M T W Th F S

I feel:
(please circle)

because because because because because

_____ _____ _____ _____ _____

_____ _____ _____ _____ _____

Today I Am Grateful For

1. _____
2. _____
3. _____

What could help transform today into a remarkable day?

Reflective Writing

How has mindfulness and meditation helped me become
more compassionate towards myself and others?

_____

_____

_____

_____

_____

_____

_____

How can someone incorporate mindfulness into daily activities?

A) Eating mindfully
B) Walking mindfully
C) Listening mindfully
D) Working mindfully

All Are Correct - Choose The Response You Feel Is Most Important
To Remember

I feel:
(please circle)

because   because   because   because   because

_____ _____ _____ _____ _____

_____ _____ _____ _____ _____

Today I Am Grateful For

1. _____
2. _____
3. _____

What could help transform today into a remarkable day?

Reflective Writing

What have I learned most from my mindfulness and meditation practice?

_____

_____

_____

_____

_____

_____

_____

What is mindful listening?

A) Ignoring outside noises
B) Focusing intently on the speaker without planning
C) Responding immediately to what is heard
D) Being fully present and attentive to the speaker

All Are Correct - Choose The Response You Feel Is Most Important To Remember

As we reach the final pages of this journey through "Positive Mindset," I want to extend my heartfelt thanks to you. Your commitment to exploring positivity and its transformative power is not only commendable but a testament to your desire for personal growth and a richer, more fulfilling life experience.

Remember, the journey towards a positive mindset is ongoing and ever-evolving. Each day presents new opportunities to apply these principles, to learn, and to grow. I encourage you to revisit these pages whenever you need a reminder of your incredible potential to foster positivity and resilience in the face of life's challenges.

As we part ways, I leave you with a quote that has been a guiding star in my journey: "The greatest discovery of any generation is that a human can alter his life by altering his attitude."

– William James.

Thank you for allowing me to be a part of your journey. May your path be filled with light, hope, and endless possibilities. Farewell, and may you carry the spirit of positivity with you, today and always.

With gratitude and best wishes,

Sensei Paul David

Reflective Writing

_____

_____

_____

_____

_____

_____

_____

_____

_____

_____

_____

_____

_____

_____

_____

_____

_____

_____

_____

_____

_____

The End

As you close the pages of this mindfulness journal, remember that each word you've written is a step on your journey towards self-awareness and inner peace. Embrace the moments of clarity, the revelations, and even the uncertainties you've encountered along the way. Let this journal be a testament to your growth and a reminder that every day offers a new opportunity to be present, to observe, and to appreciate the simple wonders of life. Carry these lessons forward, and may your path be filled with mindful moments and serene reflections. Until we meet again in these pages, be gentle with yourself and stay anchored in the now.

Mindfulness isn't difficult, we just need to remember to do it.

Thank You!

If you found this book helpful, I would be grateful if you would **post an honest review on Amazon** so this book can reach other supportive readers like you!

All you need to do is digitally flip to the back and leave your review. Or visit amazon.com/author/senseipauldavid click the correct book cover and click on the blue link next to the yellow stars that say, "customer reviews."

As always...
It's a great day to be alive!

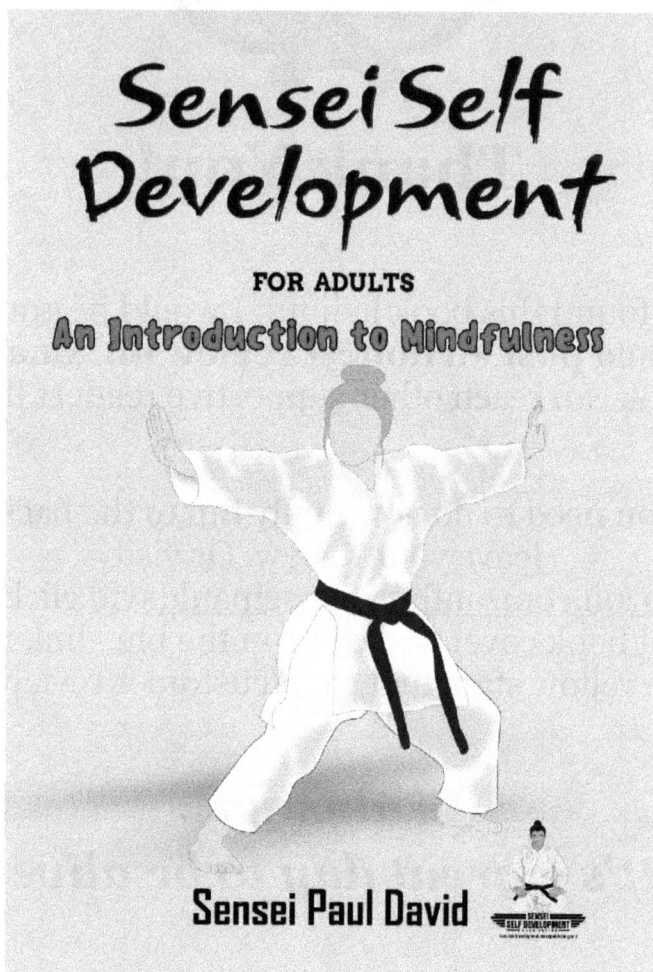

Check Out The SSD Chronicles Series CLICK HERE

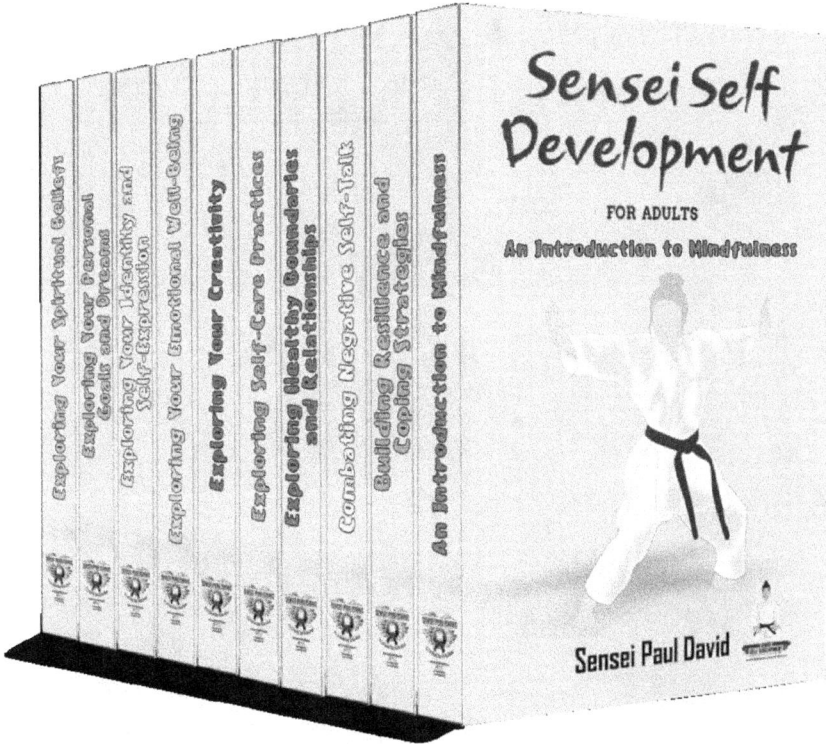

Sensei Self Development

FOR ADULTS

An Introduction to Mindfulness

Sensei Paul David

Get/Share Your FREE All-Ages Mental Health eBook Now at

www.senseiselfdevelopment.com

Or CLICK HERE

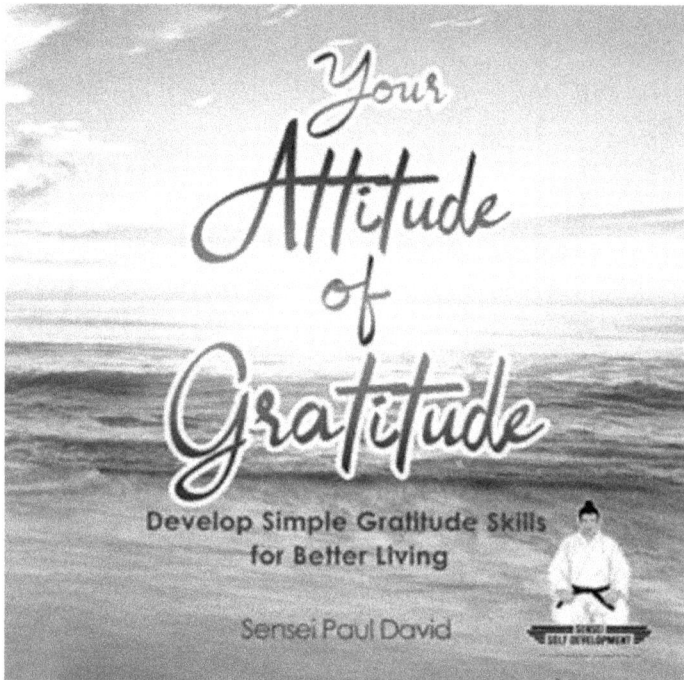

senseiselfdevelopment.com

Click Another Book In The SSD
BOOK SERIES:

senseipublishing.com/SSD_SERIES

CLICK HERE

senseiselfdevelopment.senseipublishing.com

Join Our Publishing Journey!

If you would like to receive FREE BOOKS, please visit **www.senseipublishing.com**. Join our newsletter by entering your email address in the pop-up box

Follow Sensei Paul David on Amazon

CLICK THE LOGO BELOW

FREE BONUS!!!
Experience Over 25 FREE Engaging Guided Meditations!

Prized Skills & Practices for Adults & Kids. Help Restore Deep-Sleep, Lower Stress, Improve Posture, Navigate Uncertainty & More.

Download the Free Insight Timer App and click the link below:
http://insig.ht/sensei_paul

About Sensei Publishing

Sensei Publishing commits itself to helping people of all ages transform into better versions of themselves by providing high-quality and research-based self-development books with an emphasis on mental health and guided meditations. Sensei Publishing offers well-written e-books, audiobooks, paperbacks and online courses that simplify complicated but practical topics in line with its mission to inspire people towards positive transformation.

It's a great day to be alive!

About the Author

I create simple & transformative eBooks & Guided Meditations for Adults & Children proven to help navigate uncertainty, solve niche problems & bring families closer together.

I'm a former finance project manager, private pilot, jiu-jitsu instructor, musician & former University of Toronto Fitness Trainer. I prefer a science-based approach to focus on these & other areas in my life to stay humble & hungry to evolve. I hope you enjoy my work and I'd love to hear your feedback.

- It's a great day to be alive!

Sensei Paul David

Scan & Follow/Like/Subscribe: Facebook, Instagram,
YouTube: @senseipublishing

Scan using your phone/iPad camera for Social Media
Visit us at www.senseipublishing.com and sign up for our
newsletter to learn more about our exciting books and to
experience our FREE Guided Meditations for Kids & Adults.

www.ingramcontent.com/pod-product-compliance
Lightning Source LLC
Chambersburg PA
CBHW071244020426
42333CB00015B/1617